Triplets? Relax!

Tips to Guide You Through the First Year, Sanity Intact

By Victoria Adams

Cover design by Jacquelyn McGhee

ISBN 978-0578099644

First Edition

Table of Contents

This book is based on opinion and personal experience. All information is intended for your general knowledge only and is not to be used as a substitute for medical advice or treatment.

Preface

I created this book to address the immediate needs of triplet parents during their first year. This book is designed to provide valuable information in a quick and to the point manner.

When I brought my triplets home from the hospital I realized I needed to educate myself on the daily functions of raising triplets. As I searched for information, I found the thickness and layout of most books on multiples to be cumbersome. I simply did not have time to sift through them to find the key information I needed. This book was created specifically for parents with limited time and uses a layout that is easy to reference. You now have the knowledge of an experienced mom of triplets at your fingertips.

Please note that the tips in this book are suggestions, ideas and explanations on how I addressed certain situations or obstacles. While I hope you are able to get valuable and creative information out of this book, every person and situation is different. You may have to adjust some of these tips to suit your style or needs.

Introduction

Around the time our triplets were born, a job opportunity came to my husband that would allow me to stay home and raise our babies. For me, staying home with our triplets was a dream come true. However, my husband's new job came with a demanding schedule. During the week he did not get home until after the babies were in bed. He often worked on weekends and occasionally had to go on overnight business trips.

Having one income meant spending less money, so hiring daily help was never an option. Since both our families lived hours away, I was faced with the challenge of taking care of our triplets mostly on my own. I learned how to feed them, take them to doctor appointments, and when my husband went on business trips, conduct middle of the night feedings all on my own.

I soon realized that, with a routine in place, taking care of triplets by myself was manageable. Shortly thereafter, I was able to take it a step further and take them for walks, to the park, grocery shopping, restaurants and to story time on my own. As a result, I wrote this book to share tips with other triplet parents about what worked for me during the first year of raising triplets.

Like a lot of triplets, my babies were born premature. Any age references that I make in this book are done using their adjusted age, which is used to track development for preemies.

This book will provide useful tips for taking care of triplets, and it will show new parents that it is possible to take care of triplets without additional assistance. Most importantly, it will bring you the sense of confidence and control that you will need. Let's begin the journey.

Chapter 1:

The Basics:
Set Up/Sleeping/Feeding and More

Tip 1

"Baby Zone"

My husband and I transformed our living room and dining room into a "baby zone" for the first few months. We kept our triplets in this area throughout the day and night. It served as the main hub for feeding, changing, playing, bathing and even sleeping. We set up "stations" consisting of baby swings, bouncer/vibrating chairs, play mats and bassinets/pack 'n plays. During the day, when the babies were not being fed, we would rotate them throughout the stations. At each station, the babies would either sleep or be entertained so that I was able to eat, do laundry, wash bottles, prepare bottles, rest or pump breast milk. During the night, this area allowed for us to take shifts so we could each get a five hour block of sleep as explained in the next tip.

Note: Once the triplets were big enough to sleep in cribs instead of bassinets, we moved all sleeping to their room.

Tip 2

Shifts: Sleep for the Caregivers

The baby zone served another purpose: it kept our bedroom quiet! My husband and I would assign ourselves shifts during the night to make sure that we each got a block of five hours of sleep. I would sleep from 9pm to 2am, and my husband would sleep from 2am to 7am then get ready for work. While working our shift in the baby zone, we would usually be able to get an extra hour of sleep on the couch.

On the weekends, we would rotate shorter shifts in the baby zone throughout the day so that we could get more sleep.

Bonus Tip: White noise was great for the babies' room, but it was also great for the adults' bedroom! We would run a box fan in our room to block out sound coming from the other rooms in the house.

Tip 3

Feeding Every Three Hours

In the beginning you are most likely feeding the babies every three hours around the clock. The following tips focus on how to make the process efficient so that you can create the most time for yourself in between each feeding.

1. Plan ahead - It always amazed me how hunger came like clockwork, but as soon as it was around three hours from the beginning of the last feeding, one of our babies would start showing signs that they were hungry. I had bottles already made in the refrigerator so that the only thing I had to do at the three hour mark was heat up the bottles. I would start the feeding process at the first sign of hunger. If I tried to hold them off, I would soon have three hungry babies crying. Staying on top of the schedule was important.

2. Diaper change first, feed second - This sets a routine for everyone to follow and avoids the confusion of trying to figure out if a diaper has been changed. If a baby had a bottle, we also knew they had a clean diaper!

3. Your feeding preference - You can feed all three at the same time, two at the same time or each one individually. See tip 4 on pages 10 and 11 for further instruction.

4. All three babies eat at the three hour mark - Whatever feeding preference you choose, as soon as you are done with a feeding, move onto the next baby so all babies eat around the same time. If one baby was still sleeping and it was their turn to eat, we woke the sleeping baby and fed them to keep everyone on the same schedule.

5. A second hand - If you have someone to help, assign tasks. One person can change diapers while the other person is warming up bottles and getting bibs. Then you both feed the babies at the same time using a dual feeding technique as stated in tip 4 on pages 10 and 11. With two people you can usually have the feeding process completed in 45 minutes.

Note: A sample schedule of my day can be found on pages 38 and 39.

Tip 4

Feeding Two or Three
Babies at the Same Time

If you choose to prop bottles, there are products out there that you can buy to feed three babies at the same time. I chose not to prop bottles. I felt the feeding process gave me quality one-on-one time with each baby. I either fed two babies at a time or fed them individually. Here are some techniques I used when I fed two at a time:

Bouncer chairs - Buckle two babies into their own bouncer chair, sit between the bouncer chairs and hold the bottles for them.

Boppy pillow - Can be used in a similar way as the bouncer chair. Lay each baby in a Boppy pillow so they are at an incline and hold the bottles for them.

Use your lap - You can feed two babies at a time by positioning the babies in your lap. See illustrations.

Mix it up - I would put one baby in my lap and then use the bouncer chair or Boppy pillow to feed the second baby at the same time.

| Heads resting on knees. Babies rest inside the circle created with your legs. | Heads resting on legs by hips. Legs crossed while babies rest on the outside of them. | Combination of both techniques. |

Tip 5

Laundry

If you miss a day of laundry you can start to run out of baby clothes, bibs and towels. To avoid this, my husband would throw in a load of laundry every morning before he went to work. It took him about two minutes to do, but it made a big difference for me during the day.

Bonus Tip: Believe it or not, I didn't fold baby clothes. I went through clean clothing so fast that I found it to be a waste of time. I kept a three-drawer chest (almost like a nightstand) by the changing table and filled each drawer with the clothes they wore most often. I also kept clothes, towels and bibs in short, rectangular laundry baskets. I found that these baskets fit nicely underneath the changing table.

Tip 6

Visitors

You will have many visitors. Take advantage of this. If they ask you for suggestions on what to bring to your house, a good request is to have them bring meals so you do not have to cook for yourself or others. While they are visiting, ask them to do diaper changes, feedings, and if you feel comfortable, watch the babies while you nap. If close relatives are visiting, don't be shy. They are usually willing to lend a hand with dishes and laundry as well.

Tip 7

The Must Haves

Swings - Swings can be as good as having another person lending a hand. I could usually count on the babies being quiet while they were in a swing. You will need at least one swing, but one for each baby is ideal. Babies will spend hours in swings since they provide rocking, music and something to look at like a mobile or mirror.

Bouncer chairs with vibration and hanging toys - I used these chairs everyday for the majority of the triplets' first year. I had three chairs and they were well worth the investment. The babies slept and ate in them, and they enjoyed looking at the hanging toys and feeling the vibration and bouncing. These chairs are also great for babies with reflux. The incline is at a perfect angle to reduce reflux. I also found the incline of these chairs to be perfect for teaching the babies to hold their own bottles when they were ready (about six months adjusted age for my children).

Gym/play mat - Gym/play mats are another great form of entertainment for the majority of the first year. Play mats provide different functions as the babies grow to encourage developmental milestones such as reaching and rolling over. Since the mats have pictures on them, they are also good for belly time to give the babies something to look at.

Footed pajamas with zippers - For the first year, my babies mostly wore footed pajamas during the fall, winter and spring. Footed pajamas are functional clothing that makes changing diapers or outfits efficient. My husband especially preferred the ones with zippers for nighttime feedings, when the room was dim and trying to line up snaps could be challenging.

Video monitor with multiple cameras - There are video monitors that have the capability to hook up to multiple cameras. You usually have to purchase the initial camera and monitor package then buy the additional cameras separately. I had three cameras hooked up to a handheld video monitor. It was great because I could see exactly what was going on without having to go into the room. The monitor I used was the Summer Infant Sleek & Secure™ Handheld Color Video Monitor. You can find it at http://www.summerinfant.com.

Triplet stroller - The triplet stroller makes it possible to venture outside the house without any assistance. The one I own, the Triplette SW Stroller from Peg-Pérego, has the option to take off the stroller seats and use compatible car seats that click into the stroller frame. The car seat feature made taking the babies to doctor appointments by myself super-efficient. It can be found at http://us.pegperego.com.

Binder for records - Whether or not your babies were in the NICU, there is a lot of medical information you will need to remember. I bought a large binder, created a section for each baby using dividers, punched holes in every doctor record I received and inserted the record into the correct section. Even if you stay with the same doctors/hospital from birth, some specialists don't have access to all of the records and will ask you a lot of questions. I brought this binder to every appointment during the babies' first year. An organized binder will assure you have the correct medical information.

Tip 8

Your Personal Priorities

Between feedings you will have one to two hours when you don't need to tend to the babies because they are either napping or being entertained in their station. During this time (as long as you are already set up for the next feeding), make eating and resting your first priority, especially if you are providing breast milk. Remember the saying, "You must first take care of yourself in order to take care of others."

Tip 9

When You Need a Break

There were times when the babies were crying but I found myself needing a break. Below are tips on what I did to give myself a small break to re-energize.

Play the same music everyday - I played the same group of songs everyday. Once the songs became familiar to the babies, they quieted down for most of the time the music played.

Six minutes - It sounds short, but just take six minutes of time for yourself to do something else. I would sit or lie down, eat a meal, watch TV or surf the Internet. That short amount of time was all it took to clear my mind enough to make me feel refreshed and energized.

The crib - When the babies started moving around but I needed a break, I would put them in their crib for a couple of minutes. Even if they were crying, I knew they were secure and I could get a small break.

Television - I used this as a last resort when nothing else worked. I never sat my babies in front of the TV on a daily basis. One of the benefits to only using the TV on rare occasions is that, when you do sit them in front of the TV, they become quiet because it is something they are not familiar with. I would buckle them into their bouncer chairs, line them up in front of the TV and the crying would always stop.

Tip 10

When You Need to Hire Help

Recovering from bed rest, a C-Section, and soon after that, mastitis, I found myself getting sick more often than usual. When I felt under the weather, I knew I needed help. It is a good idea to already have someone in mind who can watch the triplets when needed. Trying to find help once you are already sick is not easy. There is a fair amount of research and a meeting process that takes place before you and the person(s) hired feel comfortable. You might find that some people will not watch three babies by themselves, or if they will, their fees go up based on the number of babies they are watching. I sometimes had to hire more than one person at the same time. The best way to find sitters is to ask people you trust for referrals. Another good source is to ask the NICU nurses if they know of anyone. I soon had my list of people I felt comfortable calling. Having a few options is important; if one person was already booked, I could call the next person on my list.

Bonus Tip: The only time I hired someone was when I was sick and needed to rest. I usually got a discounted rate because I was still in the house and available. Ask about different pricing if you plan to be in the house when the sitter is there.

Chapter 2:

When Sleeping Schedules Change

Tip 1

Creating "The Schedule"

At this stage you will notice the babies are sleeping a little longer and spacing out the time between feedings. However, your hard work is going to continue because the groundwork is being set. What you do here will create "The Schedule" and make the daily process easier in the coming weeks and months. Babies like routine. Once you are on a schedule, you will live by the schedule and will start enjoying more sleep and more free time.

Note: I started this process around five months (adjusted age).

Tip 2

During the Day

Around five months (adjusted age), I started to implement a nap schedule. This included a morning and afternoon nap. Getting triplets on a routine napping schedule can be a challenge, but stick with it because it pays off. I used the "two and two" method where they would be awake for two hours, then I would put them down for a nap. When they would wake up I would have them up for two hours and then put them back down for a nap and so on. The key is to look for cues that they are tired starting an hour and a half to two hours into their awake period. Continue with that pattern until you find what times they are consistently falling asleep. In a few weeks you will have a set morning and afternoon napping schedule. This will completely change your days, giving you set blocks of time to yourself while they nap.

Tip 3

Setting a Bedtime

We started putting the babies to bed at a set bedtime each night at around five months (adjusted age). Create a routine that includes some sort of winding down activity. My routine would be to feed them, put them in their cribs, turn off the lights and play their crib soother a couple of times while I stayed in the room. We only had one crib soother and I placed it where all three could see it. It played music and provided a visual for them. After they got used to the routine, when I placed them in their cribs, I was able to play the crib soother but leave the room.

Tip 4

Waking Up in the Middle of the Night

Around three months (adjusted age) our babies were big enough to start sleeping in their cribs. We started to notice that they were sleeping longer blocks at night. Around the time I was forming a napping schedule and set bedtime, the blocks of sleep at night grew longer. Soon, we noticed that the babies were only getting up once during the night. Until this point, we had still been waking and feeding all three babies once one baby woke up and started to cry. With only one feeding in the middle of the night, we started to try techniques to get everyone sleeping through the night. For more explanation see the next tip.

Tip 5

Getting Everyone to Sleep Through the Night

There are many techniques for getting babies to sleep through the night. Since the reasons for waking up may vary for each baby, you may need to try different techniques. I have talked to other triplet moms who had all three sleeping through the night at four or five months old. I had a different experience.

Personal Story: We noticed that our two girls were waking up every night on their own, and we would have to wake our son up to feed. When we stopped waking him up for the night feeding, we found that he would sleep through the night. With only two babies waking up, feeding could be done by one person. Since my husband had to be in the office each morning, I would feed the girls by myself and let him sleep through the night. Gradually, I realized that one baby was usually the first to wake up, and if I tended to her quickly and quietly, the other two would sleep through the night.

By seven months (adjusted age), I only had one baby waking up for a middle of the night feeding. I tried many methods to get her to sleep through the night. Finally, I found one that worked. I fed her an ounce of milk less each night during the middle of the night feeding. By the time I was down to two ounces, she started sleeping through the night. By eight months (adjusted age), all three were sleeping 10-12 hours through the night.

Tip 6

Stick to Your Schedule

You now have a set schedule, more free time and more sleep. Your babies will like the routine as well, so making sure you stick to your schedule has benefits for everyone. At this stage missing a nap can throw the whole day off. You will also start to notice that the babies are entertaining each other in their cribs. You might hear them talking and laughing before they go to sleep and after they wake up.

Chapter 3:

Breastfeeding and Pumping Breast Milk

Tip 1

Breastfeeding

I did a combination of breastfeeding and pumping for six months. Due to continuous clogged milk ducts and a bout with mastitis, I ended up strictly pumping until my crew was 14 and a half months old (chronological age). For some, breastfeeding just clicks. For others, different techniques or aids such as nipple shields may need to be used. If breastfeeding works for you, there are special pillows designed so you can feed two babies at the same time. If breastfeeding is a challenge but you want to breastfeed, keep trying and keep them familiar with the process. My infants weren't good at breastfeeding until they were a few months old. This was even after drinking from a bottle. It just took time for them to get it.

Note: Although the rest of the tips in this chapter focus on pumping, it may benefit you to read them because you may be able to incorporate these ideas with breastfeeding.

For those wondering, my babies received some formula from time to time to make up for what I wasn't able to produce.

Tip 2

Pumping Breast Milk and Multi-Tasking

I would feed a baby (see tip 7 on page 37) or eat a snack while I was pumping. It also served as a time to wind down or de-stress. Because pumping would force me to sit down, I would end up relaxing and watching television or reading a magazine during that time.

Tip 3

Pump Attachments

You probably own one set of pump attachments for your pump. Do yourself a favor and invest in two or three sets of attachments. I owned three sets. It is worth the money to invest in more than one set so you don't have the added demand of having to wash the attachments after every pump. I would put my attachments in soapy water until all three were used and then wash them all together. Having more than one set of attachments also allows you to keep up with pumping during your block of sleep as explained in Tip 9 on page 40.

Tip 4

The Portable Pump

For the first few months I was using a pump from the hospital. Hospitals and drug stores offer rentals for the large hospital-grade pumps. These are good options if you are not sure how long you will pump or if you are trying to build your supply. However, these large pumps really tie you to wherever they are located. It wasn't until I ventured into the pumping section at our local store that I saw the freedom that portable pumps could bring. They are small enough to use in the car or restroom and can be carried with you wherever you go. If you plan on pumping for awhile, this might be a good investment. Just know that there are options and you aren't locked in to the equipment the hospital uses.

Tip 5

Pumping and Your Supply

One piece of advice I got from a nurse sums it up: "What you pump today will be what you get tomorrow". This means that with pumping there is a delay, but if you keep it up you will see results. If you pump every two hours today, you will see a low volume, but tomorrow you will see the results.

Tip 6

Increasing Your Supply

Women with singletons are mostly told to pump for 10 minutes every three hours. With triplets, I was advised by my lactation consultant to pump for 15 minutes every two hours. With this schedule, I was able to get a good supply. I pumped every two hours around the clock. When the babies started sleeping longer through the night, I started to play around with the time and frequency of how much I pumped. I found that pumping for 20 minutes gave me two "let downs", increasing my volume. I was also able to start spacing out the time between pumping to every three hours. If you are trying to increase your supply, try adding time on to each pumping session to see if you can get multiple let downs.

Tip 7

Pumping While Bottle Feeding Technique

To be as efficient as possible, I was able to pump while I was bottle feeding a baby. Here is the explanation on how this technique was accomplished.

- I found that 6 oz. bottles attached to my pump pieces were the perfect height for the bottles to rest on my legs.

- I would sit with my legs crossed (criss-cross applesauce style!).

- I would put a baby in my lap and bottle feed.

- Leaning slightly forward for the 6 oz. bottles to rest on my legs allowed me to be hands free and pump while feeding a baby at the same time.

Bonus Tip: There are products out there for the purpose of hands free pumping. They look like thick fabric belts that you can insert the pump attachments into. I know some women for whom this product worked great. Due to clogging milk duct issues, I was not able to use this product effectively. However, there are many options that can be found by typing in "hands free pumping bra" at www.amazon.com.

Tip 8

Sample Schedule

Here is an example of a typical day with feedings every three hours.

8:00 am - Pump while feeding baby A.

8:30 am - Feed baby B.

9:00 am - Feed baby C.

9:30 - 10:00 am - Eat, wash bottles, housework, etc.

10:00 - 10:15 am - Pump (eat, watch TV, read).

10:20 - 10:50 am - Housework, rest, etc.

10:50 am - Start warming bottles for the 11 am feeding and prepare bottles from the fresh milk pumped at 10 am.

11:00 am - Feed baby A.

11:30 am - Feed baby B.

12:00 pm - Feed baby C and pump.

12:30 pm - 1:50 pm - Housework, rest, etc.

1:50 pm - Start warming bottles and for 2 pm feeding and make bottles from fresh milk that was just pumped.

2:00 pm - Start next feeding and pump.

This would go on until the first sleep shift. If my husband was able to arrive home from work by 7 pm we would tend to the babies together for two hours and then I would start my sleeping shift at 9 pm. The schedule was very regimented, but this was what I found to bring balance and efficiency to the day. Feeding each baby separately was good bonding time. Hopefully you can use some ideas from this schedule to create what works best for you.

Bonus Tip: If you have leftover breast milk and plan to reuse it for the following feeding, you can mark the outside of the bottles with a dry erase marker or use baby bottle bands. You can find many options at www.amazon.com.

Tip 9

Pumping During Longer Stretches of Sleep

One common concern women have is keeping up their supply and getting sleep without missing a scheduled pumping session. If you are on a schedule that has you pumping every two or three hours, but you have a five hour block of sleep scheduled, how can you make sure you don't miss that scheduled pumping session? Below I describe how I kept on schedule during my block of sleep.

This schedule is a continuation of the sample schedule on page 38 - 39.

8:40 pm - Pump.

9:00 pm - Go to bed.

10:40 pm - Pump. I woke up to an alarm clock and I had the pump set up next to bed with the attachments in place. The only thing I had to do was sit up, put the pieces in place and turn on the pump. After 15 minutes, I placed the pump pieces with the milk in them into an insulated bag that contained ice and fell back asleep.

1:45 am - Wake up and pump. I had a second set of attachments with me in the bedroom for this pump.

2:00 am - My shift with the babies started.

Chapter 4:

Money Saving Ideas

Tip 1

Freebies

Depending on the age of the book or article you are reading, you may hear a lot about companies that will send you free items if you send them a letter and a copy of the triplets' birth certificates. Through various resources I compiled a list of such companies. I sent letters to each and found out that a number of the companies had discontinued their multiples program. Some companies directed me to their Web sites, where I could find coupons. From what I found, the only companies that were worth the time I put into sending letters were the food, formula and diaper companies. From these, I received cases of formula or manufacturer's coupons. If you are interested in contacting companies for free items, focus on the formula, food and diaper companies first because you will at least receive items worth the time and the stamp.

Bonus Tip: To receive free products from companies that have multiples programs, the products must be claimed before the babies turn one.

Tip 2

Open Only What You Need

As hard as it might be, it's best to refrain from taking all your new gifts and purchases out of the packaging and taking the tags off all the cute new baby clothes. Only take items out of the packaging and remove tags as you need them. Because family members and friends can be very generous, you may find yourself with more articles of clothing and baby related items than you could ever use. Before you know it, the babies will have grown out of unworn clothing, or you'll find that you never had a use for some item. Keeping items with tags or original packaging may allow you to make returns or exchanges for more useful items. This includes diapers that you may need to exchange to get the next size up. Of course, save all your receipts, including gift receipts.

Tip 3

The "Gently Used" Market

Look to purchase items and clothing from the "gently used" market. A lot of baby clothing being resold is in great condition since many articles only get worn a few times. There are many places to shop including online, garage sales, thrift stores, or your local multiples club; many hold bi-annual sales. Go to http://www.nomotc.org/ to find out where your local clubs are located.

Tip 4

Your Used Item Has Value!

Try to sell or swap items once you are finished using them. There are so many options for selling items. Post online, hold a garage sale, go to a thrift store (they buy or swap items) or join a multiples club that holds bi-annual sales for the public.

Tip 5

Keep All Original Packaging

When you are taking baby gear out of packaging and boxes, keep the original packaging. Anything that has original packaging usually looks better to the buyer and is more likely to sell versus the same item that doesn't have the packaging.

Tip 6

Always Think Ahead

When you are at a thrift store or garage sale and see something in good condition at a good price, buy it even if the babies are not old enough to fit into the item. When people ask you what size the babies wear, ask for the next size up if they already have enough clothes in their current size. You will start to compile a lot of quality items to use in the future, and you'll get good deals while doing so. Thinking ahead also takes away the stress of making sure the babies have clothes that fit when their sizes change. Once a size started getting tight, I could just open a box of clothing I was storing in the next size.

Tip 7

Call the Manufacturer

When something breaks, call the manufacturing company. Even if you bought the item used or it is no longer under warranty, I found that the company would sometimes send me a replacement for free. I had pump valves tear, a stroller part and a swing break, and toys that had paint coming off. Don't spend a dime until you address it with the company. Think of the money a simple phone call can save you!

Tip 8

Parts for Sale

If something is broken and the manufacturer will not replace the item for free or at a cost that is worth it to you, there are still options. Internet sites like eBay often have parts for sale that you can buy and use to fix the item yourself.

On the other hand, if you no longer need the item and fixing it isn't of value to you, think about selling its parts individually. In the example of the swing, the manufacturer was going to send me a replacement motor that I would have had to pay for. I was no longer using the swing, so I decided not to fix it. However, I was able to sell the swing cover, tray, etc. individually on eBay.

Not into selling/buying parts online? You still have one more option. Every now and then Babies "R" Us stores have trade-in events where you can swap your used item for a discount on a new item (there are guidelines to this trade-in). This means you can take your broken swing and trade it in for a discount on a new car seat, pack n' play or whatever you might need at the time.

Tip 9

The Library

This resource may be obvious to some, but a lot of people forget the value of a public library. Instead of buying books and music or paying for a class, look into what your library system offers. Libraries today are like community centers! You can take out books, videos and music for kids. Our local library offers story and activity time. Don't forget to look past your own library branch and into what the whole library system (all branches) offers. Different branches often hold different programs. For example, the branch one town over from where we live offers music and yoga classes which we are able to attend.

Bonus Tip: Looking for more to do? Look into local kid gyms and places that offer classes specifically for toddlers. These places usually offer at least one free trial class.

Tip 10

Rewards Programs

You will get offers from diaper, formula and toy companies to sign up for their rewards programs. At first it might seem that all you are getting is more mail and emails. However, keep scanning your rewards cards, entering codes and signing up for these programs because they have value. Many businesses will contact you through these programs and offer you free items or services. I have received coupons, gift certificates, a free 20 page photo book, 50 free prints and four free classes to a children's gym.

Bonus Tip: Babies 'R' Us has a multiple birth discount program. They offer customers 10% off two or more of the same items purchased in the same order (i.e. two cribs, two bedding sets, two strollers, etc.). The discount applies to certain categories. You can contact your local store for more information.

Chapter 5:

The Next Stages

Tip 1

Always Changing

Keep in mind that babies grow so fast in the first year that things are always changing. You may have your feeding routine down, and then they start solid food. Just as you get the hang of that, they start sitting up and you have them in high chairs. Before you know it, they are transitioning from bottles to cups. Keep to a schedule but make adjustments within it so the schedule grows with your children.

Tip 2

Gated Play Area

As our children grew and started rolling across the living room floor, the "baby zone" transitioned into a "play zone". Our main floor had an open layout so we added a colorful plastic gate with eight panels that could be linked together. Having this gated area helped me stay in control while giving the triplets a safe place to play. It was one of the best investments I have made. As the babies grew and needed more space, we were able to add more panels and even attach the gate to a wall to make a rather large area for the kids to walk and run around in. One other amazing feature it had was portability. We took it on every trip we made. It broke down into separate panels and we would take about five of the panels with us on trips. The gate I owned was a very heavy plastic that stood on its own even if it wasn't connected or attached to the wall. It was heavy enough that the kids couldn't lift it, get under it or knock it down. We really had no issues until they turned one, when they learned to climb over it. Until that point, the gated area provided a space for the triplets and their toys, and it allowed me to run to the bathroom or throw in a load of laundry during the day without worry. It also created a safe zone when we went to other people's houses.

The gated area also allowed us to focus on one baby at a time. When they started walking we could take the babies out of the gated area one at a time and supervise them while they roamed around and explored.

Note: Although I secured the gate so the babies couldn't go under it or knock it down, there was a point where they started to find ways to go over it. For me it didn't happen until after they were one, but you'll want to keep an eye on their activity.

Tip 3

Holding the Bottle

Once they were picking up and holding toys, I figured they could hold their own bottles and started to teach them this skill. I buckled them into their bouncy chairs, which put them at the perfect incline. I put their hands around the bottle and I supervised to make sure the bottle was kept in place. It takes practice, but they soon understood how it worked and started holding the bottle on their own.

Tip 4

Distract with Toys

Once the babies start reaching, holding toys or rolling over, they may no longer lie still on their backs during diaper changes. Give them a toy or something safe to hold and inspect. This worked for my babies even over a year old. I just gave them something more challenging the older they got.

This tactic also came in handy when they were playing. The art of distraction can be a good way to solve an argument when they want the same toy.

Bonus Tip: I put a small toy inside the paper box that held the diaper cream and closed the box. The babies would lie still on the changing table trying to get the toy out of the box. If they started twisting and trying to get up on the changing table, I would offer a toy or book that they haven't seen in a while. I kept a basket of toys and books on top of the three-drawer stand that held their clothes so I had options.

Tip 5

Making Your Own Purees

One day each week (usually Sunday), I would cook food (meat, vegetables) for the week, puree and freeze it. You can freeze purees in ice cube trays or little baggies, or buy one of the many products out there designed for freezing pureed food. You can go to www.amazon.com and type in "freeze baby food" for lots of different options.

Bonus Tip: Pureeing food is simple. Take your cooked food, put it in a blender or food processor and add water until you have the desired consistency.

Tip 6

Transition to Straw Cups

Getting the babies completely off bottles by the time they are one is important, so I planned ahead. Instead of using sippy cups, I went straight to cups with straws to avoid having to make two transitions. I also thought that sucking from a bottle was similar to sucking through a straw and that the transition would be easier if I avoided the sippy cup altogether. Once the triplets were able to sit up in their play area, I would put a straw cup with water in the play area for them to explore, and soon they were taking sips on their own. When we were finally ready to make the full switch from bottles to straws, the process was almost seamless.

Tip 7

Traveling

We took a few overnight trips and long car rides with the babies before they turned one. Here are some tips that worked for us.

- Plan to make stops for diaper changes, feedings and stretching for you and the babies.

- Keep the same schedule for naps, feedings, and bedtime.

- Make sure you bring your nap and bedtime routine with you. If you use white noise or read a certain book, bring it. You want to do everything you can to simulate their routine at home.

- If you own a gated play area, bring panels from it with you.

- If you are using infant car seats (seats with carrying handles that are designed to be taken in and out of the car), they work well as seats for feedings. You want to pack as little as you can. If you use convertible car seats instead of infant car seats, see tips 10 and 11 on pages 66 and 67.

Bonus Tip: For our stops, we looked for an open public area like a school playground, church or park and laid down a blanket. We spent our time during stops doing diaper changes, feedings and allowing the kids to play. We would put down a heavy, reusable plastic table cloth underneath our blanket in case the grass was wet. It kept our blanket dry and clean.

Tip 8

Electrical Outlet Covers

Believe it or not, many places that are geared toward children do not think to cover their electrical outlets. I have been to the pediatrician's office, the children's room at the library, portrait studios and many other places that have infants in them every day, and the outlets were exposed. When my kids reached a certain age, they were running around in these rooms. Sometimes I had to park the stroller next to an outlet. I purchased my own outlet covers (the kind you just push into an outlet) and carried them in my diaper bag. When I saw an exposed outlet, I just plugged it with one of my covers. I paid a few dollars for the covers, and it was a smart investment to avoid this safety hazard.

Tip 9

Teaching Patience

Around the time the triplets turned one, I realized I was still going at high speed when it came to feeding, and each baby would cry if they didn't have their food in front of them immediately. I realized it was time to teach patience. I sat all three in their high chairs, made them wait until I had everyone's food ready and then put their food in front of them at the same time. They learned to wait and they weren't crying or grabbing at each other's food because they all got the same thing at the same time.

Tip 10

High Chairs to Booster Seats

Some parents skip high chairs altogether and use a triplet feeding table or booster seats with trays. I used high chairs lined up next to each other and would spoon feed all three kids out of the same bowl using the same spoon (unless there was a sickness in the house). I chose high chairs mainly for their reclining ability, which was useful when the babies were still using bottles. However, once the kids were not drinking from bottles or eating purees anymore, I wanted us to sit down together and have a meal at a table. Around the time they turned one, I moved them from the high chairs to booster seats around the table. Although there was still a lot to do at mealtime, I did try to eat my meals with them. Sitting down with them and having a meal together has become a favorite part of our daily routine.

Bonus Tip: If you buy booster seats, look for ones that travel well and fold up so you have the option to bring them with you when you travel.

Tip 11

Eating and Drinking Equals Sitting

Breakfast and snack time were quick, simple meals for us. I gave the triplets breakfast and snacks in their play area while I sat with them and supervised. From the time I started this, I enforced that the kids had to sit down while they were eating or drinking. It is safest for them to be sitting while eating and drinking, but it also comes in handy when you are not at home and don't have their feeding seats.

Tip 12

Your Community

Here is some information on organizations, clubs and assistance you may want to look in to.

The Triplet Connection – www.tripletconnection.org

The Triplet Connection

P.O. Box 429

Spring City, Utah 84662

Phone: (435) 851-1105

Email: tc@tripletconnection.org

Raising Multiples a MOST Community (FKA Mothers of Supertwins) – www.mostonline.org

PO Box 306

East Islip, NY 11730-0306

Phone: (631) 859-1110

Email: info@mostonline.org

Twins Day Festival, Twinsburg, Ohio – www.twinsdays.org
This festival is known for being the largest annual gathering of twins & other multiples in the world. The festival is open to all multiples.

Multiples of America (AKA National Organization of Mothers of Twins Clubs) - http://www.nomotc.org - is a network of more than 320 local clubs representing over 25,000 parents of twins and higher order multiples. Look online at www.nomotc.org for your information on your local club.

Early Intervention - This is a state program that provides family-centered services to help children who are at risk (i.e., preemies) of developmental delays or disorders. Contact your state or county offices, or talk to someone at your hospital or pediatrician's office to get more information.

Preemie clinic / Neonatal follow-up - This is for families with babies that were born premature. The hospital where you delivered most likely has a program where the NICU doctors follow the babies' growth and development for at least the first two and a half years.

Preemieprints.org - http://www.preemieprints.org/ - Through their network of volunteers, Preemie Prints gives NICU families no charge professional photography. They provide free photo sessions and digital images to families with babies in the NICU or NICU graduates up to 1 year of age.

In Closing

Thank you for taking me with you on your journey of the first year of raising your triplets. I hope you found the information in this book to be useful and that you are able to apply some of the tips to your everyday life. While the format of this book is quick and to the point, please note that these tips and techniques did take practice and patience. Nothing happens overnight.

I have found that making the everyday functions efficient has allowed me time to play and relax with my kids. Over time you will find what works for you, but hopefully this book has allowed you to do some out-of-the-box thinking to bring in a little creativity on how you can make your days flow.

I am sure you have heard this a lot, but make it a point to take lots of pictures. The first year is so memorable and full of changes. Soon you will find yourself taking your kids to the park, going to story time or just sitting down and having a meal together. Step back and take it all in because you now have the confidence and control that this book talks about. All you need to do next is have a good time with your triplets and *relax*!

Made in the USA
Monee, IL
10 December 2020